KINGDOM CONTRACT OF TOTAL COMMITMENT TO THE LORD JESUS CHRIST, KING OF Kings AND LORD OF Lords *

I hereby totally surrender all that I have and am, or shall ever have or be, completely to Jesus Christ, and I invite Jesus inside of me as Lord, forever.

(All other conditions and terms of this contract to be filled in later, subject to the guidance and direction of Jesus Christ.)

_____
_____
_____
_____
_____

Date: _____

Witness: _____
Signature: _____

*Note:
This is an eternally binding legal contract!

The KING'S GREATEST SECRET!

by
John Roy Bohlen
and
John 5:30

Copyright © by John Roy Bohlen

This edition is lovingly dedicated
to wife Karen, & our family.

Entire reproductions of this message are encouraged. You are hereby given permission to copy, record, print, teach, preach, zerox, fax, share, memorize, recite, handwrite, dictate, read, film, CD, DVD, type, or by any and every other means, get this word out to as many people as possible, in as many places as possible, as quickly as possible, by as many means and methods as possible.

You are commanded by God to teach this secret to others in the Great Commission.

Matthew 28:18-20

"These things that you have learned and received from me, commit thou to faithful ones who shall be able to teach others also."

II Timothy 2:2

Library of Congress Catalogue
Card Number ISBN # 0-9697702-4-0

Published by, for, and in behalf of the Kingdom of God.

GREAT COMMISSION MINISTRIES
9473 County Road D,
Webster, WI 54893
715-866-4060 • gcmco77@yahoo.com
www.Great-Commission-Ministries.org

TABLE OF CONTENTS

The King's Greatest Secret! 9
Mount Popokatapetel, or "The
   Long-Distance God" 15
The Secret! 16
You Are Beautiful !!! 19
Victory Verses 19
The Road To Hell Is Paved
   With Good Excuses 21
Monstrous Manichean Madness 25
How Long Can You Live Without Sinning? . 28
If God Didn't Make Little
   Green Apples In Minneapolis 29
Crisis and Process 32
Are You Ready To Die? Then Live......... 33
The Greatest Moment Of My Life! 35
3 Steps To Take 36
"The Life That Wins!" 38
Cataclysmic Revolution 40
Are You Filled With God, Right Now? 42
"Little Boy At The Baptism" 44
The 4th Coming Of Christ?!?!?! 46
Inferiority Complex 50
The Elephant and The Grasshopper 52
A Bee In Your Bonnet................. 54
The Glory Spell 54
The Foundation Stone 54
The Illustration of the Cross & The Mirror . 57
As Christ Is, So Are We - In This World! ... 60

ABOUT THE AUTHOR

John Roy Bohlen is like no one else I have ever met. He is absolutely "unhindered" in his relationship with the Lord. He is the only man I know who regularly goes outside in the middle of the night to watch the stars. The thought that the same God Who created the stars, lives, as John likes to say it, "between my ears and behind my eyes" thoroughly captivates him.

John has served in many different capacities in the Body of Christ. But that is not why I listen to him. John is an honorary high chieftain in Nigeria - a country he has visited many, many times. But that is not why I listen to him. He has written many books and articles that have been a great help to many people. But that is not why I listen to him. It is not his credentials that impress me. I don't think they impress him either. The Lord impresses him. And that is why I enjoy and listen to John Bohlen. He knows my Master. He knows Him well. And when you spend time with John, whether in one of his books or in person, he makes sure you come face to face with Jesus. Jesus' Life literally spills off of John.

I am excited that you have this book in your hands. If you read it and believe it, your life will be changed.

Tom Kelby
Hands to the Plow Ministries

COMMENTS ABOUT JOHN BOHLEN

John Bohlen is a person of unquestioned integrity who has dedicated his life to the fulfillment of the Great Commission.

John's message about "The King's Greatest Secret" has blessed many throughout the United States, and his books are in great demand in Africa as well as in the United States. In the opinion of many, John is one of the foremost authorities on the concept of the Kingdom of God.

John is an active speaker who has blessed audiences in four continents with his Spirit-led message about Kingdom principles, Kingdom living, and what the Kingdom of God really is.

My wife and I have had the privilege of contributing to The Great Commission Ministries and feel that it has been a good investment in the spread of the Gospel of Jesus Christ.

- Robert Benedict,
President,
Resource Development Consultants

THE KING'S GREATEST SECRET !!!

Introduction

A SECRET! The GREATEST Secret! God's Greatest Secret! The best Secret you could know! But, almost no one knows this Secret! That's why it's a Secret! God kept it a Secret, until just the right time! Now is the time! You may be one of the very first to get in on the Secret - until now, one of the very few. The Bible calls it "The Mystery of the Gospel of the Ages"! Mystery means "A Secret"! Gospel means "Glorious Good News"! Since this "Secret" comes from the KING of Kings, I call it…

"The King's Greatest Secret!"

If you learn this "Secret",
God promises that you will "live happily ever after"!
God promises that you will live "The Overcoming Life"!
God promises that all of your days will be merry and bright!
God promises you happiness and success.
God promises you
great fulfillment,
lasting accomplishment,
great personal satisfaction,
peace that passes all understanding,
joy unspeakable,
full of glory,
life eternal,
riches untold,
fullness of joy,
and pleasures forevermore!!!

IF YOU GET THIS "SECRET"!

If you get this "Secret"! When I tell you this "Secret", you may be tempted to say, "Oh, silly, I already know about this." But, do you know that less than 1 in 10,000 born-again believers knows this "Secret"?!. This "Secret" is also a "Mystery". This is why you will need to pay close attention, and pray especially that God will help you solve this mystery, and help you learn this special "Secret"!

Let me ask you a quick question that will help you know whether or not you already know this "Secret". Quickly list the most important things that Christ Jesus took of yours with Him to the Cross. Most Christians will rightly say, "Yes, He took my sins, so I can be forgiven." A few more will rightly answer, "Yes, He took my sicknesses, so that I can be healed." ***Please stop for a moment, to answer this question.***

WARNING!

Jesus prayed a strange prayer: He "rejoiced in Spirit" and prayed, "I thank You, Father, Lord of Heaven and Earth, that You have hidden these things from the wise and prudent (of intelligence, discernment, and learning), and have revealed them unto babes, (the child-like, the simple, the unskilled), for so it did seem pleasing in Thy sight." Matt.11:25 & Luke 10:21 Amp.

Can you imagine Jesus and the Father getting a kick out of telling a "Secret" that children or mentally challenged people understand, but that remains hidden from the smart, educated, wealthy, or wise?

There is a strange and mysterious quality about this "Secret". It can stand in plain sight for all of a person's life, and one might never get the "Secret". As we said, less than 1 in 10,000 Christians knows this "Secret", even though it is in plain sight, in the New Testament, which means that there is small chance that you will know this "Most Important of Secrets!". It is even possible that you will still not know the "Secret", even after you read this little book. We have done our very best to make this "Secret" plain, but God has packaged this "Secret" in such a way that you must really pay attention, and sincerely ask God to make this mystery plain and understandable.

Everything that we have and are from God is BY HIS MERCY, GRACE, PITY, LOVING KINDNESS, TENDER MERCIES, LOVE, GRACIOUSNESS, GOODNESS and CONDESCENSION - every heartbeat, every breath, every good thought, every kind deed, everything we give to God or others - "God has worked in us, both to will and to do of His good pleasure." Phil.2:13 And this is no exception. This grace must be coupled with your intercession - if necessary, we encourage you to beg God, and plead with Him, with thanksgiving, that He graciously grant you to know - this "SECRET". We encourage you to seek God, very respectfully, with great persistence - until God graciously, in His great love for you, reveals it to you.

Here it is then:

**THE
KING'S
GREATEST
SECRET
!!!
!!**

"THE KING'S GREATEST SECRET!"

God has a "Secret"!! He would like to tell it to you! The angels and men of God wanted to know this "Secret", but God wouldn't tell them for thousands of years. Then God told "The Secret" to the Church through the Apostle Paul and the other apostles and prophets. That "Secret" was lost and forgotten again during the dark ages, but now is being told again in this special time to the Church. It's "The King's Greatest Secret!" It needs to be told, so very much. Almost no one in the Body of Christ, today, knows the "Secret". We have ministered in many churches across the world, and in most of them, we ask a certain question to find out if they know "The Secret". In very few of these places where we have ministered, did they know. The question we asked them was, "What did Jesus take of ours, with Him, to the Cross?" *Will you take a minute to answer this, before you continue?*

We get answers, all of them correct, but not complete, such as, "He took our sins, our sicknesses, our worries, burdens, fears, etc." We say, "That's true, that He took these, so we can be forgiven, healthy, and without worry (some folks cast their burdens upon Yahweh, the Almighty Right NOW God, but as a fisherman casts, they sit and reel these burdens back to themselves.) But these people still have not told the main thing Christ took with Him to the Cross! I suppose the reason they do not know, is that it requires a revelation of God, or one who has a revelation from God, to share "The Secret" before they can know. What a Wonderful Mystery!

MOUNT PO-PO-KAT-A-PET'-EL

We believe that more than 9,999 Christians out of 10,000, relate to God in one of the following incorrect ways:

1) They relate to God "long distance". That is, they envision God as living way out beyond Mount Popokatapetel somewhere, and that, if they pray real long and loud and hard, that maybe, God will hear them, and that, maybe, but less likely, that answer will come back. An old song says that Jesus leans out over the battlements of Heaven, and yells down the distance, " 'Hold the fort, for I am coming' - Jesus signals still. Wave the answer back to Heaven, 'By Thy grace, we will'."

2) The other incorrect concept of God, (we shall see, in a moment, why these are incorrect) is that

of a "little bitty God living inside of a BIG person, with still **BIGGER** problems". We invite Jesus to come into our hearts, and so He does, not as our very LIFE, in most cases, but as a sometimes-thought-of "Guest". (I don't like, nor will I say that prayer, "Come, Lord Jesus, be our Guest . . ") I don't want Him to be a "guest". I want Him to come in as the Resident President, the Master, my very Lord and LIFE!!! But, some of us, when we pray to Jesus, hiding down deep, in some corner of our lives, somewhere, we get our own echoes back as if we were talking into a well. But, God wants to be very, Very, VERY much more real to us than this!

As my friend, Chuck Dodge, says, "God has a consuming desire to make Himself real to us, and to live His Life through us. In order for Him to really become our Life, we need to relate to Him correctly; and in order to relate to Him in a really healthy way, we need to know 'The Secret'!"

THE "SECRET"!!!

"The Secret" is found in plain sight, in a multitude of places in the Bible, especially in places like John 17, Ephesians, Romans, Galatians, Colossians, etc. BEWARE that when you hear this "Secret", that you do not think too lightly or casually. The proof that you got "the Secret" will be that you will be able to consistently keep your heart and attitude and spirit right. In fact, if you REALLY get "the Secret", as the following Scriptures indicate, there will be no difference between Who Christ is, at the Father's right hand, and, Who He is, - - - in you!!!

"The Secret Mystery" is this: When Christ went to the Cross, He took US with Him there! When He died, WE died! When He was buried, WE were buried with ALL of our insufficiencies, inferiorities, inadequacies, insecurities, inabilities, instabilities and dysfunctions. Everything negative, nasty, weak, or sinful about us, Jesus took to the Cross, because He took US to the Cross!! Oh, Dear One, if you grasp hold of this "Secret", it will make the difference between you living your life, and Christ living your life; between you trying to speak good things, and Christ speaking His words through you.

Lord Jesus, please make this Mystery plain and understandable to me. We believe together, that You will make the Mystery clear. "I praise Thee, O Father, Lord of Heaven and Earth, that

Thou didst hide these things from the wise and intelligent, and didst reveal them to babes. Yes, Father, for thus it was well pleasing in Thy sight!" (Matthew 11:25 and Luke 10:21)

Please let me tell you more about "The Secret!". When the Lord Jesus Christ went to the Cross, He took you with Him there! YOU WERE THERE when they crucified my Lord! Christ looked ahead into the present time, and saw you, and decided that He could not help you any other way, that He could not beat or bless you into being what He wants you to be, could not educate you or "religious" you adequately, but that the only hope for you was to take you with Him to the Cross, and kill you dead, along with all of your negative nature and qualities, and bury you! Unlike many self-help books, Christ does not try to get you to "hype" or hypnotize, "con" or convince yourself into thinking that you are really good or nice, adequate or O.K., but that you are horribly hopeless and hideously helpless, apart from Christ taking you to the Cross with Him, and putting all of your self to death and burying it in the tomb with Him. So, you do not need to kill yourself or commit suicide, nor do your friends, because Jesus Christ lovingly killed us softly, already. But that is not the end of the story!

YOU ARE BEAUTIFUL !!!

When Christ rose from the tomb, HE RAISED YOU UP as a whole, new, beautiful, wonderful, adequate, sufficient, glorious, superior, perfect, able, stable, secure creation in His Image, in newness of Life, so He can come into us, and BE our Life, live our Life, BE our perfection, BE our righteousness!!! Jesus is NOT interested in helping us live the Christian life. No, NO! Christ wants us to allow Him to live His Own Life, in and through us!! Jesus does not want to help us think good thoughts, say good words, or do good deeds. NO! Jesus wants to think His Own thoughts through us. Christ wants to say His Own words through us!! Will you let Him?

Perhaps you would like to see this "Secret" in the Bible. Because of this "Secret", the following verses can become attainable in the practical realm of the nitty gritty, right now:

1 Cor.15:57	Victory
2 Cor.2:14-16	Victory, always, everywhere
Rom.6:6-22	Free from sin
Col.3:1-3	Risen with Christ our Life
Eph.2:6	Seated in Christ
Ps.16:11	Fullness of joy

1 Pet.1:8	Joy unspeakable
Ps.91	Secret Place of the Most High
Eph.1:3-4	Every blessing
Neh.8:10	Joy of the Lord, our Strength
1 Cor.2:16	Mind of Christ
Phil.4:13	Can do all things through Christ
Jude 24	We can walk blamelessly
Mt.28:18	All power and authority
Mt.5:14	We are the light of the world
Phil.1:21	To live = Christ
2 Cor.9:8	All, all, always abounding
John 14:13	Whatever we ask
John 10:10	Abundant Life
2 Pet.1:1-4	All things for Life
Rom.8:37	More than conquerors
1 John 4:17	We are as He is
Mt.19:26	All things are possible
Luke 8:10	Know the mysteries of the Kingdom
1 John 2:6	Walk as Jesus walked
Col.1:25-29	Greatest Mystery in History
1 Cor.1:30	Christ IS my Wisdom, my Salvation
2 Cor.3:18	I can look like Jesus

Galatians 2:20 says, "I have been crucified with Christ, and it is no longer I who live, BUT CHRIST LIVES IN ME!!!" In Colossians, God

says that CHRIST IS OUR LIFE! The Bible says, "For me to live IS Christ" (1 Cor.2:16), and "As He (Christ) is, **SO ARE WE** in this World" 1 John 4:17. Oh, Dear Heart, I pray for you with deep, unutterable longing and faith "That the God of our Lord Jesus Christ, the Father of Glory, may give you The Spirit of Wisdom and of Revelation in the Knowledge of Him! I pray that the eyes of your heart may be enlightened so that you may KNOW..." (Eph.1:17-20).

Our son, Joshua, points out here, that if you really get this "Secret", that most of your deepest questions will be answered, as Jesus is the "Yes" of God. (2 Corinthians 1:17-20).

THE ROAD TO HELL
IS PAVED WITH GOOD EXCUSES

Do you realize that if God Himself stepped down from a fluffy white cloud and offered an easy way for us to be consistently victorious, that many Christians would simply not be interested?! The "Good News" Message, (that we can walk before the Lord, consistently pleasing in motive, thought, word and deed), would be, to many "Christians", very "bad news". A major reason is that they want an excuse for their sinning! Another reason is that they would have to change their "doctrine", and, when it comes to doctrine, some folks would rather go to Hell, than switch!

I have gone from door to door, trying to persuade people to invite Jesus Christ into their hearts as their Lord and Savior, as a necessary FIRST step in escaping the eternal flames of Hell, but instead, they most OFTEN answer, "Look, I've got my own _____ . I was born a _____ . I was raised a _____ . And, I am going to die a _____." Most of them might as well have added, "And, I am going to go to Hell, as a _____." Church membership does NOT give a person entrance into the Kingdom of God, but only by being born again, as Jesus declares in John 3:3-5, and Revelation 3:20, where He tells us how: "I am standing at the door of your life, and I am knocking. If you will invite Me to come into your life and heart, as Savior King of Everything, then I **will** come in." That's how to be born again! Will you invite Jesus to come in, right now?!

But, after we're born again, it's very important that we don't begin making excuses for not measuring up to God's will for us, because, contrary to what we may have been taught, there is **no** excuse for not doing the will of God! I have often wondered what would have happened in the Garden of Eden, if Adam would not have tried to make excuses, when God came and asked him why he "messed up". Instead, Adam said, "The woman!" Then, he added, "Whom YOU GAVE to me . . ." I wonder what would have happened if Adam would have said, "Lord, please don't blame Eve. Let all the blame be upon me. She's the weaker vessel, and I should have been looking out for her." Or, what if Eve would have said the same? Instead, she blamed the whole thing on the serpent. The only good thing I can think of to say about the devil, is that, when God came to him, he didn't pass the buck or try to place blame. Never mind the fact that he didn't have any place to pass it! But it is impossible for us to be both EXCUSING and REPENTING at the same time. God will NOT forgive what we are excusing. Most Christians have been brainwashed, hypnotized, or otherwise programmed into thinking that "nobody's perfect". The excuse, "I'm only human after all ..." is typical, but definitely counterproductive. Remember, the Lord gives, in His Word, many victory promises: 1 Corinthians 10:13 says that, "There is NO temptation taken you but such as is common to man: but GOD IS FAITHFUL, Who will NOT let you be tempted above what you are able, but will, with the temptation, make a way for you to escape, that you may be able to bear it." And, in 2 Corinthians 2:14, "Now, thanks be unto God, Who ALWAYS causes us to TRIUMPH IN CHRIST, and makes manifest the savor of His knowledge by us in EVERY place." This means:

"Victory = Always-Everywhere!!!"

Romans 8:37, "In ALL THESE THINGS, WE ARE MORE THAN CONQUERORS THROUGH HIM That loves us!" And, Philippians 4:13, "I can do ALL things through Christ, Who strengthens me!!!"

But, so many of us, if we were honest and consistent with our own system of unbelief and wrong doctrine, have CHANGED these very Victory Scriptures to read OTHER THAN what God has actually said!!! We have tended to say, "No! God has NOT given me a way to escape!" or, "NO! God does NOT cause me to triumph in every place and circumstance!" or, "NO! I am NOT more than a conqueror in all, or even, in very many of these things!" or,

"I am not even a conqueror, much less, <u>more than</u> a conqueror."

Intricately interwoven into the fabric of our thinking, is some wrong doctrine that has been spuriously spread throughout nearly all of Christendom. Protestants and Catholics, EVERY denomination - it seems that hardly anyone has been spared. This doctrine of the dualism of nature, concerns our attitude toward our bodies, toward pleasure, our flesh, perfection, victory, - towards Life, itself! A fresh revelation realization of "The King's Greatest Secret!" changes all this.

MONSTROUS MANICHEAN MADNESS

The Church was fully free of faulty thinking in this area, until about the fourth and fifth century after Christ, when a funny, but phony philosophy of "dualism" infiltrated the Church, from a man called "the father of Christian philosophy and theology". He introduced a warped way of thinking into the Church that was not corrected by the theologians or philosophers that were to follow. Here is the man, the doctrine and the correction to his approach.

St. Augustine, 354-430 A.D., was a Greek Manichean philosopher, prior to his coming into the Church. Here, we quote from the World Book Dictionary: *"Manichean (man' e ke' en) - n, a member of a Gnostic Sect, arising in Persia in the 200's A.D., compounded of Christian, Buddhistic, Zoroastrian, and other beliefs, and maintaining a theological dualism, in which the body and matter were identified with darkness and evil, and the soul, striving to liberate itself, was identified with light and goodness."* In other words, while God's Hebrews believed matter and the body to be good or bad, depending upon the use to which it was put, - the Manichiests believed and taught that the body itself was evil, and that everything that the body did, or was, or said was only always exceedingly sinful. Sound familiar? Nearly every church and catechism and liturgy we know of, has something of this within it. Some have even given the illustration, that, inside every person, there is a white dog nature and a black dog nature, and that the one that wins is the one you say "sic 'em" to (or feed), the most. That's what we mean by "dualism".

Instead, God's Hebrews properly said that matter, a pen, a human body was not bad in itself, but that its inherent goodness or evil was determined by what one **did** with that matter, or pen or human body. This is why, in Romans 8, Paul says that "the instruments of our body are slaves of righteousness if we yield them to do righteous things, and that they are instruments of unrighteousness if we yield them to do unrighteous things."

But the Manicheans said that the members of our body are bad, because they were made of substance, of material, of matter. So, in Augustine's writings, he says that it is a sin to watch a dog chase a rabbit. Why? Because the body gets all excited and involved, and says, "Let's see now, is the dog gonna catch the rabbit, or is the rabbit gonna catch the dog?" Augustine said, "I have learned to take my food as medicine." In other words, he disciplined himself to the place where a big juicy piece of beefsteak tasted like cod liver oil, just so his body would not get all involved, excited, and sinful. My well rounded Mother told me one time, that every act of sex is sinful. (She had four grown children!) She quoted David's verse, "I was born and conceived in sin." She didn't know about David's personal family situation. I said, "Mother, what a terrible thing to say about us kids."

The real question is NOT, "Can I keep from sinning?", but, "Is God great enough to keep me from sinning?!" Is He? If someone asks me, "Do you ever get a wrong spirit or attitude toward your wife or children or anyone?", or, if they say, "Don't you ever sin?", I respond, "I don't recommend it!" or, "We're not in favor of it." If they argue, "Do you actually think a person can get through the day without sinning?", I respond, "We'd advise it."

If you admit that you do not sin, they will call you a liar. But if you say you do sin, they will say, "See there! It's not possible to keep from sinning!"

Mark Twain allegedly wrote in his memoirs, *"Went to church today. Preacher preached on sin. Only problem was, Ah couldn't rahtly tell whether he was fer it, 'r again' it!"* You know, sometimes a body can't tell by looking at some Christians' lives and doctrines, whether or not they're in favor of sin, or against it, either!!

HOW LONG CAN YOU LIVE WITHOUT SINNING?

1 John 1:9 says that "If we confess our sins, God is faithful and just, - and will cleanse us from (not "some", or "much", or "most", but) **ALLLLL** unrighteousness." Let's say

that you just "1John 1 nined it". How much unrighteousness do you have left in you? Doesn't it say "allllll"?! How long can you stay cleansed from all unrighteousness, through the power of God, and by the Strength, and through the Life of God lived through you??? 5 seconds? 5 minutes, by God your Strength? 5 hours, through Christ your Power? 5 days, with Christ as your Life? 5 decades, with Jesus Christ AS YOUR RIGHTEOUSNESS!!!!?! Please remember the former list of victory Scriptures we gave earlier. Or, would you rather continue on, in your excuse-making and sinning?

IF GOD DIDN'T MAKE LITTLE GREEN APPLES IN MINNEAPOLIS

There is a false doctrine called "sinless perfection" that teaches that we can reach a state in this life where it becomes impossible for us to sin. We are **NOT** teaching this false doctrine. However, there is another equally false doctrine, which teaches that "we cannot keep from sinning"! Please carefully note the difference:

Lie # 1: "Impossible to sin" = "Sinless perfection".

Lie # 2: "Impossible to keep from sinning" = lie of the devil.

THE TRUTH: "Possible to NOT sin!!!" Given the POWER of God, and the Grace of God, and the Spirit of God, and the Life of God, and the Word of God, and the blood of Jesus, and the King's Greatest Secret, etc., etc., etc.

Paul, in Philippians 3, uses the word "perfect" in two different ways. In verse 12, he says he's not perfect, and in verse 15, he says that he IS perfect!! I wonder why we only always hear that he is NOT perfect, and never hear that he IS perfect??! Imagine, if you will, a little green apple, just barely past the blossom stage, a little bitty nubbin of a thing. But it's perfect! No worms, germs, dust, rust, must, crust, or crushed. It's not dashed, bashed, crashed, slashed, hashed, mashed, gashed, lashed, trashed, or gnashed. And, now, can you picture a perfectly perfect apple that's ruby, ruddy, rosy, red, ripe and juicy? If it were any more ripe, it would be rotten. And if it were any less ripe, it would be sour and woody. Please ask yourself this question: "What particular things are necessary for a smaller apple's growth and development into this mature apple?" Are bruises, or worms or tears or woundings necessary? But, is "hanging in there" necessary? The endurance of the long, cold nights? - The hot summer days, the wind, the rain?

Some folks seem to think that rebellion, backslidings, detours, lapses, luke-warmness, wrong attitudes and spastic silliness are all necessary to our growth and development in God. There IS a discipline, but it is a discipline that pertains to the new person or new man in Christ Jesus, and not the old man, or the old self or nature. The old life HAS BEEN crucified with Christ - NOT "is being" crucified. We do not believe in beating the dead carcass. That would be wasted effort, and futile. Romans 6.

So, we see that the "flesh" is neither good nor bad, in or of itself, BUT, depending upon the use to which it is put. Adam, before he fell, had flesh, and our redeemed bodies will be flesh. Even Jesus had flesh! Hebrews 5 speaks of Jesus, "Who, in the days of His flesh - - offered up prayers with strong crying and tears - - and - - though He were a Son, yet He learned obedience through the things which He suffered. And BEING MADE PERFECT, He became the Author of Eternal Salvation unto all them that obey Him."

Wasn't Jesus already perfect? Of course! But here we see that He also needed to "become perfect"! Can we be perfect, in the 1 John 1:9 "cleansed from ALL unrighteousness" sense? Of course!

But, we also need to become perfect in the ripe apple sense of "growing in grace and in the knowledge of the Son of God" and in the sense of Paul's pressing "toward the mark for the prize of the high calling of God in Christ Jesus" - the fulfillment of our adventures and destinies and callings in God!!!

Good news! We can be totally forgiven now, and the power of God and His Life within can KEEP us pure, but we can grow in increasing levels of faith and love and encouragement. Our increasing appreciation of God and His creation need never cease!!

CRISIS AND PROCESS

So, there is both a crisis and a process to every experience that we are to have in God: the New Birth, the Lordship of Christ, Sanctification, (dedicated and made holy), the Holy Spirit, etc.

Ask some "Christians" if they are saved, and they'll say, "I dunno, I'm workin' on it." (The Bible says we can KNOW! 1 John 5.) But because they are always "working on" the process of salvation, without the CRISIS of having been born again, they won't be - -, because they are always GOING THROUGH the door, but never quite get IN. But one can ask others if they are saved, and they say, "Ya sure, you betcha! I got saved 90 years ago"! But, too many of them got saved, and then, they got stuck! They got through the door and then went to sleep for 89 years. The same thing is true of the Holy Spirit. Some believe only in the process of being filled, while others got "it", and got stuck, or sprung leaks! And the same thing is true of the "King's Greatest Secret" - BOTH the crisis of appropriation AND the process of abiding in Him - moment by moment, both are necessary.

ARE YOU READY TO DIE? - THEN LIVE!!!

You simply: # 1) KNOW YOURSELF TO HAVE BEEN CRUCIFIED WITH CHRIST" (Rom.6:6 "KNOWNG THIS"!! - this is the crisis), (Many people do not KNOW that they "**have been** crucified with Christ"!!) and, then, # 2) Then "CONSIDER AND RECKON YOURSELF (here is the process) AS DEAD INDEED UNTO SIN, SELF AND satan, but alive unto God through Jesus Christ our Lord!!! (Rom.6:11 ALLELUYAHWEH!!! (Note: To "reckon" means, "to act like it is true, because it IS true"!)

Please repeat this prayer:

Thank You, Dear Lord Jesus, for taking us to the Cross with You, and for raising us up with You in newness of Life in You. Lord God, we receive You to BE all that You are, in us, now and forever more. We receive You AS OUR VERY LIFE, to BE OUR VERY LIFE!!! Please now, LIVE YOUR VERY LIFE THROUGH ME!!! In Jesus' Name. Amen.

Jesus said, "BE YE THEREFORE PERFECT, EVEN AS YOUR FATHER IN HEAVEN IS PERFECT." Mat. 5:48. Do you think that Jesus was joking or kidding when He said this? Jesus, as always, meant just what He said! He meant "BE as perfect as God the Father!!!" Or, would you prostitute and change and twist and warp and noneffectualize the Word of God, here, or any other place?

It does NOT mean: "try to be perfect", nor, "be perfect sometime after your body has rotted', nor, "give up on being perfect", nor, "it's impossible to be perfect", nor, "be theoretically (or 'pretend') perfect, nor any of that kind of silliness. "Would be" disciples of the Kingdom, WON'T BE disciples of the Kingdom of God, as long as they are messing with the commands of the King of

God's Kingdom, in this way! One who changes the commands of the King is a Kingdom anarchist and traitor.

When someone asks, "What does this verse mean?", the best answer always is, "The Bible, this Verse - means just what it says!!" because the King means what He says. I believe that whenever people disagree about a Scripture, it is because one or more of them are not willing to accept what the Scripture and the King says.

THE GREATEST MOMENT OF MY LIFE!

In November, 1960, my friend, Patty Troug at Bethel College told me, "John, as long as you are calling 'idealistic', 'unattainable', or 'theoretical', what God calls 'necessary', 'practical', 'available', and 'attainable', YOU are calling God a LIAR!!!" I had thrown away a book from me in disgust, <u>FOREVER TRIUMPHANT</u>, by Heugel, in which he quoted 2 Corinthians 2:14, "Thanks be unto God, Who, in Christ, ALWAYS causes us to triumph, and manifests Christ through us in EVERY place" (JB) "Victory, at ALL times and in every place! I had said, "that's too idealistic", but, then I realized, as a result of Patricia's gentle rebuke, that I had been calling God a liar, in that

He had said, "Victory, **always** and **everywhere**." And I had said, "impossible". I did not want to call God a liar any more, so I went to my room, got out my Bibles: KJV, AMP, Goodspeed, Greek N.T., etc., and laid them out on the bed, and got down on my knees in order to see just what God DID say. Sure enough, God said, "Perfect victory, always - everywhere", AND "More than conquerors", AND "Abundant Life", AND "Joy unspeakable", AND, "Full of glory", AND, "We have the Mind of Christ", AND, "Christ, our Life", AND, "Whatever we ask", AND, "Greater works than these, shall you do", AND, "I can do all things through Christ", AND "With God, all things are possible", etc., etc., etc., etc. All these Bibles said the same thing!! So, I decided to do three things:

1) **Confess** every known sin, including having called God a liar;
Please note: If you cannot remember a time when you specifically invited Jesus Christ to come and live on the inside of you, please do this NOW! That's how to be born again!!!

2) **Yield** COMPLETELY to the Lord Jesus Christ. I told the Lord Jesus that, if it were His perfect will, I would be willing to be sick, maimed, killed, single, celibate, persecuted,

misunderstood, forgotten, married to anyone He said, (I was sure He was going to make me marry somebody really terrible. But, as it turned out, God later gave me the very best!)

I ask people, "On a scale between 0 and 100, what percentage are you completely dedicated to Christ?" Then I ask them, "If God gave to you an umbrella, and it is raining, and you are only holding the umbrella over 80% of your body, will you get wet?" They say, "Sure!" Then I ask, "If the umbrella is fire-proof, and it is raining fire, will you get burned?" Then I explain to them that God will assume 100% responsibility ONLY for that percentage of our life that we give to Him. We will need "good luck" on the other 20 percent. This is why, sometimes, that bad stuff happens to good people, because God was not assuming responsibility to provide, protect or empower that percent of our lives that we refused or neglected to give to Him. Then, can we blame God? If God gives me weapons of warfare with which to tear down strongholds, and I fail to use those weapons, can I blame God if the strongholds remain? 2 Cor.10:4

Now, these two steps (confession of sin, and the dedication of my life), I had done many times before, but I carefully did them again. In fact, we should always keep up to date with the Lord, staying free from sin, and staying in a totally yielded state.

3) **Appropriate** by faith, the highest level walk in God's Spirit, with Christ AS your Life! Invite Jesus Christ to come in to your life, and actually BE your Life, and to LIVE HIS LIFE through you, from the inside out, and take over completely as your Saviour, Lord and Life!!!

Charles Trumble, in <u>The Life That Wins</u>, says that "on this third step of faith, every thing now depends". He suggests that we take a step of faith, with total disregard for the presence of (or lack of), accompanying signs or proofs, feelings or emotions, because the "transaction must be based on faith", rather than some feeling or tingle, etc. So, I remember reaching out my hand to the Lord God and saying,

"Lord Jesus, I believe You have a walk for me that I haven't been experiencing; a relationship and an experience with You that I haven't had before. Lord Jesus, I don't know what to call it, and I don't know how to get it, but, whatever You call it, and however one gets it, I receive it from You now, in cold, blind faith, not

depending on outward feelings or 'signs', as the proof of the transaction. Thank You very much. In Jesus' Name. Amen."

Can you guess what happened? You guessed it. Nothing. Outwardly, or on a feeling level, that is. I felt really dead. Oh, I had invited the Lord Jesus to come and live within me, and I had accepted the Lord Jesus as my personal Saviour, many years before, and I had yielded my Life to Him, many times before. But the same thing had happened to me, as would have happened in the Old Testament if one would have taken a clean lamb and sacrificed it under the hot Israel sun - and that's all. Can you imagine the mess? The sacrifice NEEDED the fire of God to come from Heaven to light upon and consume the sacrifice as a sign of acceptance and anointing. I rose from my knees, in faith, really sincerely believing that a genuine transaction (this third step) had taken place, yet feeling nothing.

I put away all my Bibles and climbed wearily into my top bunk. After I was settled down, I thought, "If anybody asked me to praise the Lord, right now, it would be like someone asking me to praise a haystack." That was how UN-emotional I felt, yet, I knew that I had made a genuine transaction of appropriation with God. But I was really tired, and had no positive emotions.

CATACLYSMIC REVOLUTION

Anyway, no sooner had that thought crossed my mind, about praising a haystack (indicating the lacking emotional level of positive feeling), when Christ BECAAAAME my Life!, and I have never been the same, since! It seemed like a great dam broke on the inside of me, and there came explosively gushing over me, and through me, and to me, and from me, and upon me, and around me, from deep within, and from high above, came the Glory of God, and the Joy of God, and the Love of God, and the Spirit of God, and the LIFE of God, and the Peace of God, and the Presence of God, and the Strength of God, the Anointing of God, and the Effervescent, Flooding, Overflowing Fullness of the Living God!!! I have never been the same! I felt (and feel) like a towel in a modern washing machine, the water and soap representing God, saturating, covering, washing over and through my entire being, inside and out! This year marks half a century, for me, that I have lived in this King's Greatest Secret!, and it is still just as exciting!!!!!!!

Fabulous! Incredible! Joyful! Invigorating! Beautiful! Astounding! Healing! Wonderful! Marvelous! Satisfying! Life-changing! Lasting! Miraculous! Christ BECAAAAAAME my Life! I came to see myself as having been crucified with Christ, dead and buried with Christ, RISEN, AND REIGNING WITH CHRIST JESUS in newness of Life, and seated IN Christ AT the Father's right hand, far over and above EVERYTHING that is named, in Heaven and on Earth, and GLORIFIED IN HIM - Jesus Christ! This is described in Eph.2 and Col.3, Rom.6, and Rom.8, Eph.3, 2 Cor.3, Gal.2, etc., etc., etc. (Time out - for a Glory Spell and a happy dance! Would you like to dance with me?!)

Note: From the Amplified Bible, Eph. 3:19b - "That you may be filled (through all your being) unto all the fullness of God - (that is), may have the RICHEST measure of the Divine Presence, and become a body WHOLLY filled and flooded with God Himself." I like to put it this way: "May you allllways be fillllled with allll the fullllness of God!!" Peter says, "Having become PARTAKERS OF THE DIVINE NATURE" and Colossians says, "When CHRIST, Who **IS OUR LIFE**" - - -, and "For, in Him the whole fulness of the

Deity (the Godhead, continues to dwell in bodily form - giving complete expression of the Divine Nature. And you are IN HIM, made FULL, and have come to fullness of Life - in Christ, YOU, TOO, are FILLED with the GODHEAD: Father, Son, and the Holy Spirit, and reach full spiritual stature - - -!!! (Amplified Bible).

This is what is known by various terms, such as "The Second Blessing", "The Fullness of the Spirit", the "Baptism in (of) the Holy Spirit", the "Transformed Life", The "Exchanged Life", "Walking in the Spirit", and, "Abiding in Christ". We call it, "The King's Greatest Secret!"! Col.1:27 calls it "The Mystery of the Gospel of the Ages!!"

The question for all of us, no matter what we call it, or whatever our theological background is: Are you FILLED WITH GOD, RIGHT NOW?? Jesus said, "He that believes in Me, out of his innermost being, shall gush forth flooding torrents of Living Water, continuously." Is this where you are in your walk with God? Is this what you are experiencing? This is for you!!!

Question: Are you full of God and His Holy Spirit, right at this moment? Are you up-to-date with Him and on excellent terms with Him right now? Do you minister and share from the "overflow", or, are you like a "small handful of water, in a big empty barrel". John 7:38 Amp. Pray with me?

Dear Father God: Thank You for providing unlimited anointing and every blessing and having "given us all things that pertain to life and godliness." I ask You to BEEEE and become my Life. Please, be ALL that You ARE, in me, from now on. I reckon and consider my old life to be dead. I receive You AS my "Wisdom, Righteousness, Sanctification, and Redemption". Please BE my Perfection. Love through me. Speak Your Words through me. Think Your thoughts through me. Come and walk around in my shoes. Come and wear my skin, smile through me, relate to people through me. Come and live between my ears, behind my eyes, inside my brain, my blood, my cells, my bones, my muscles. Come and live Your Life through me, always, all the time, in every place, to every one, in every situation. Pray through me. Thank You, Almighty Papa Yahweh Right Now God. I believe, from now on, that I can do ALL things through Christ my Life, and that nothing shall be impossible IN YOU!!! In Jesus Yahshua's Name. Amen.

I am over 70 years of age. If I were to take all the things I have learned in my life, all the sermons I have heard, all the education I have had, my doctor's degrees, my high chieftaincy, all the fastings, all of the times I have read the Bible through, all the pastoring and counseling we have done, all the adventures and experiences I have had: if I had to reduce it all down to one hour of teaching and truth, it would be this little book. And, if I had to reduce it all down to one sentence, it would be this:

"There is nothing more to do, than to relax, in the loving arms of my Heavenly Father, and let Christ live His glorified Life, through me."

BAPTISM

There is a true story of a little boy who was looking intently into the baptism tank, after the baptism service, when his mother came up and asked him what he was doing. He said, "I'm looking for that 'old man' the pastor said we left in the water!" You see, this is the true meaning of baptism by immersion - our total identification of actually going with Jesus into His crucifixion, death, burial, resurrection, ascension and glorification. In other words, we

need to have a powerful, on-going, gut-level revelation that we actually went with Jesus in all of these experiences, in that **we truly went WITH CHRIST** into His crucifixion, His death, His burial, His resurrection, His ascension and His glorification. The Bible declares this! Won't you accept and believe it?!

THE FOURTH COMING OF CHRIST!?!?!?!!!

A friend of mine was in a church meeting, when someone died. There was a nurse present, who verified the lack of heart-beat and breathing, the bodily functions ceased, the color of death was present. The people continued to worship intensely while the ambulance was coming. About 15 to 20 minutes later, the man opened his eyes and lived a wonderful life. His granddaughter had had a dream, two weeks earlier, that her grandfather was going to die in church, and that he would come back to life.

Assume with me for a moment, that God wants to return to the Earth in a FOURTH way. He came as a Baby, (First Coming), and He's coming in the Clouds (Second Coming), and He comes to live on the inside of us, when we become born-again, (Third Coming - Revelation 3:20 "I WILL come in!") But, now, please pretend with me, that, in addition to all of this, He wants to come in a fourth way. Imagine with me that, this time, He wants to do it like this: Suppose someone is sitting in the church, and has a cardiac attack, and dies, God forbid. Instead of rushing to give the person "artificial rescuperation", that the rest of the people, if they notice at all, think that that person just fell asleep for a minute. Suppose that before anyone else knows of this, your spirit has left your body and has gone away to the Father, while Jesus decides to come to the Earth in an new way - He leaves the Father's Throne-Room, comes down into the church, and takes up residence within your body, and BECOOOOOMES your Life!!! Before any one else is aware, Jesus comes into your newly warm dead body, blinks open your eyes, gives a little smile to others, stands up, walks around in your shoes, wearing your clothes, greeting people, loving people, speaking to people through your available body, living His glorified Life - through you, in disguise, incognito, in you, talking, loving, LIVING His LIFE - through you, the very Life of Christ, Himself!!!

The Jehovah's Witnesses believe in the First and Second Coming of Christ, but do not believe that Jesus, as God, can come and live inside of us as our Life. Because they don't believe in this Third and this Fourth Coming, they are going to a Hell that they also do not believe in.

Jesus wants to be glorified and magnified now, IN all who believe!! Notice this Scripture! "When He shall come to be glorified IN His saints and to be admired IN all them that believe" 2 Thes.1:10. "Christ IN YOU, THE HOPE OF GLORY" Col.1:28. The KJV calls it "the MYSTERY which hath been hid from ages and from generations, but NOW is made manifest to HIS saints. To whom God would make known THE RICHES OF THE GLORY OF THIS MYSTERY AMONG THE GENTILES, WHICH IS - - - <u>CHRIST IN YOU</u>, THE HOPE OF GLORY!!!"

The Williams translation calls this, "God's Glorious OPEN SECRET = CHRIST IN YOU!!! and, Beck's Translation says, "THE GLORY OF THIS HIDDEN TRUTH = CHRIST IN YOU!!!" I have called this, "The King's Greatest Secret!" This is none other than what The Creator King of Everything, in the Bible, calls "THE MYSTERY OF THE GOSPEL OF THE AGES"!!! In other words, this is the GREATEST GOOD NEWS SECRET OF ALL TIME!! Please, dear Dear One, please do NOT let this truth pass you by! Please stay with this, until this "Secret Truth" becomes nitty-gritty, gut-level REALITY IN YOUR HEART. IN JESUS' NAME. AMEN!

So, back to the illustration: Say that Christ came into your available dead body and BECAAAAAAAAAAME your Life THROUGH you, loving THROUGH you, talking, loving, walking, loving, living, loving, blessing, loving, healing, loving, BEEEING ALL THAT HE IS - IN YOU, - BEING your Salvation, NOT giving you Salvation, as an experience APART from Him, but living it, Be-ing it, DO-ing it, through you!!

1 Corinthians 1:30 says that Christ, "IS MADE unto us Wisdom, and Righteousness, and Sanctification, and Redemption". These things: Resurrection, Salvation, etc., are not a "thing", or an "experience" apart from Him, but are a PERSON. That Person's Name is YAHWEH YAHSHUA, The Almighty Right Now God, the Lord and Savior, Jesus Christ!!! Even in the Old Testament, please notice all the times it refers to Yahweh as BEING our Sword, our Shield, our Fortress, our Buckler, our Exceeding Great Reward, our High Tower,

"I will run into Him, and be safe!!" Not, "gives us a sword", but, "IS MY SWORD"!!! Dear Heart, please - can you see the difference??!

Some people come staggering into church on Sunday morning, to get their "weakly" (weekly) injection fix of righteousness to last them barely till next Sunday, but Jesus wants to BE our Righteousness!!! Be our LIFE, our Salvation and Protection. Salvation is not a "thing". Salvation is a Person! And His Name is Jesus Christ! As 1 John says, "He that has the Son, HATH Life, and he that hath not the Son of God hath not life."

INFERIORITY COMPLEX

They tell about a man who was down at the altar praying, "Lord, show me that I am nothing, show me I'm nothing." Someone came along and said, "Take it by faith, brother." Story is told of a man used to have a terrible bad inferiority complex. Then, somebody came along and told him he didn't have an inferiority complex, he was just plain inferior! As a teen-ager, I used to do things constantly to compensate for my deep-seated feelings of inadequacy. The ol' one room country school we went to was called "Wild Cat" School. Then, we went into town to the citified junior high school, and, truth to tell, I didn't rightly know how to act around those city-wise kids. So, to try to do something about my inferiority complex, I thought maybe I could get a good book of advice from the school lie-berry. The first book I got said, "Act natural". But that didn't help much, you see, because I knew that the thing that I naturally was, I could not afford to publicly be! So, I got another book, and it said, "Be yourself". But that didn't help either, because MY old self definitely WAS inferior! Later on, my friend, Lee Eliason, told me to "Be sincere", and that helped some, but here, as a senior at Bethel College, my discovery of this "Greatest Secret" fully met the needs of my life, along this line, because Christ Jesus BECAAAME my Sufficiency, and my Adequacy!!!!! This really, Really, REALLY solved the "complex" problem. 2 Cor. 3:5-6 tells us where our adequacy, our sufficiency is to come from. It says that "our adequacy (sufficiency) is from God, Who also made us adequate (sufficient)"!!!

Therefore, you do not need to die or to commit suicide - because Christ wants to BECOME your LIFE by your acceptance. Accept what He did when He took NOT ONLY our sins and sicknesses, so we can be forgiven, saved, and healed completely, but He took our SELVES. (Rom.6,

Col., Eph., etc.) Jesus put US to death with Him, along with ALL of our inabilities, inferiorities, inadequacies, instabilities, insufficiencies - everything negative, nasty, weak and sinful. He took us to the Cross, put us to death with Him, Everything dysfunctional and negative about us, our sinful nature, our old man, our Adamic nature: crucified, killed, dead and buried! Then Christ raised us up with Him in newness of Life, as a whole, new, beautiful, glorious, adequate, able, stable creation, fashioned in His Image in newness of Life, that Christ is now available to come and live His gloriously victorious Divine Life through us, and BECOME OUR VERY LIFE!!!!!!! Will you ask Him? Will you allow Him, Jesus, as God, to live His glorified Life through you, 24, 7?!!!!

THE ELEPHANT AND THE GRASSHOPPER

The story is told of an elephant who had a friend who was a grasshopper that rode around behind the elephant's ear, so they could talk. One day they came to a jungle bridge. When they crossed it, the bridge shook and swung and swayed. After they crossed the bridge, the grasshopper yelled into the elephant's ear, "We sure shook that bridge, didn't we!" And, at

the end of each of our days, we can whisper into the ear of God our Heavenly Daddy and Friend, Papa Yahweh, "We sure shook our world, today, didn't we!!" Jesus Christ, Creator King of Everything, wants to live His glorious Life through us, every moment, magnificently!!!

A BEE IN YOUR BONNET

I was counseling with a 70 year old woman who had had problems. But, then, she had a "glory spell" when I told her about "The King's Greatest Secret! She said, "I was born again and baptized in the Holy Spirit when I was 10 years old, and have been walking with God, ever since. But in all the years I've walked with God, I have never once heard these truths, that Christ can actually BEEEEE my LIFE!!" When a person truly comes to know this wonderful "Secret", then the transformation in a person's life should be just as great as if Christ Himself actually BECAAAAME that person's very LIFE!!! Interested? Interested in helping us share with others, this "Secret"??! Please share this "Secret!"

THE FOUNDATION STONE!

This "Secret" is so very, very foundational to virtually every other truth in Scripture! For example, with regard to prayer, we must believe for Christ, Himself, to be on location, praying His prayers through us, by the Holy Spirit, according to the will of the Father. With regard to miracles or a ministry, we are to believe that Christ is on location, ministering and being that ministry through us. We want Jesus to BE the parent through us, BE the spouse!!! Say it, again: "Jesus wants to live His Life through you!" This is precisely how to live every aspect of the Christian Life! Christ does not want you to try to live the Christian life. Jesus wants to BEEE your Christian Life, to Live through you!!

We can have an experience GREATER THAN if we had a heart attack, and Jesus Christ came into our newly dead body and started living in the Earth, disguised AS US, because, better than this CAN BE OURS by simply accepting that we were crucified with Christ, already, on the Cross, in order for Him to LIVE HIS LIFE IN AND THROUGH US!!! We must accept the fact that He put us to death with Him on the Cross, in order to do this very thing - so Jesus could come and live His Life through us. Now, Christ wants to BE all that He is, in us, and Be His righteous Self, through us. If Jesus IS our righteousness, we will be as righteous as the Heavenly Father, simply because Jesus is as righteous as the Father!! Remember, Jesus said in Mt.5:48, "BE YE THEREFORE PERFECT, EVEN AS YOUR FATHER IN HEAVEN, IS PERFECT"! That's how we do it. Simply reckon the old life to be dead, (Rom.6) and receive Christ, not only inside to BE your Saviour and Master and total Lord, but also, BEING all that He is, in you, as your very Life!!! Are you ready?!

Jesus wants to walk around in YOUR shoes, wearing YOUR clothes, speaking HIS words through you, praying HIS prayers through you, thinking HIS thoughts through you, blessing HIS people through you, loving, healing, encouraging others, through YOU!!! Jesus wants to BE the Parent of your children, through you. He wants to be the spouse of your spouse, through you! Jesus wants to be the Neighbor of your neighbor, the Worker on your job, a Leader in your church, the Changer of your world, THROUGH YOU!!! Jesus wants to be the Establisher of His Kingdom, through you. He wants to Rule the World - through you! Jesus wants to heal people, the Binder and Loser of situations, the Fulfiller of the Great Commission - all through YOU!!! ALL THIS CAN BE YOURS, FROM NOW ON, AS YOU ALLOW JESUS CHRIST TO ACTUALLY LIVE HIS

GLORIFIED LIFE THROUGH YOU, YOU, YOU, YOU!!! Will you let Him, allow Him, Jesus to live through you?

1 John 4:17b tells us that God wants there to be NO DIFFERENCE between Who He is, at the Father's right hand, and Who He is, in You. If you have any questions about this, please leave no stone unturned until you know deeeeep within your heart - - - this "Greatest Secret" of the King. If you cannot get this "Secret" through reading these words, and carefully praying your way through the Scriptures listed, then, please get in touch with us - because this MUST become absolutely workable and practical in your life! This is the KEY, literally, to EVERYTHING you are, and are to be, in God.

THE MIRROR AND THE CROSS

Instead of a crucifix, I've often thought of having a cross with nothing on it except a mirror, as a reminder that "you were there, when they crucified my Lord"!! Jesus actually took you with Him on the Cross, and you were there with and in Him, "when He rose up from the Tomb"!!! Galatians 2:20, Romans 6, 2 Cor.3:18, etc. Here it is, then - God's "Greatest Secret"! Christ, living His Glorified

Life in you, through you, AS your Life!!" JESUS CHRIST WANTS TO ACTUALLY BE YOUR LIFE!! JESUS WANTS TO LIVE HIS GLORIFIED LIFE THROUGH YOU, RIGHT HERE, RIGHT NOW, FROM NOW ON, ALWAYS!!!

What would happen if Jesus came to the Earth to live in disguise in someone, before coming in the clouds? What if He came to live His glorified Life in Your town? Your family? Your church? Your factory? Your skin? Your marriage? Your shoes? Your clothes. Your brain. Well, That's exactly what God wants to happen!! Exactly! NO DIFFERENCE!! Christ - YOUR LIFE!

Will you pray with me now, very sincerely, very earnestly?!

"Lord God of the Impossible, now and always, please come and be made all glorious in me, and marveled at in me. I believe, Lord God, I believe for You to come and live Your Glorified Life - IN ME!! I ask You, Lord Jesus, to come into my heart and life and BEEE my Saviour. I receive You as my Lord, and as the Commander and Boss of my life. I thank You for taking me with You to the Cross, to

the death, to the grave, and to your Throne-Room. I consider and reckon myself to have been crucified with You, having died with You, having been buried with You, along with alllll of my inferiorities, inadequacies, spasticities and insufficiencies. And then, Jesus, You raised me up with You in newness of Life, as a whole, new, beautiful, glorious, adequate, able, stable, sufficient person in You, that You are now welcome to live Your glorious Life through me, from now on, moment by moment, from here to Eternity!!! I believe and receive the Truth that there is nothing more for me to do, than for me to simply relax myself in Your loving Arms, Papa Yahweh, Father Daddy God, and then simply allow You, Lord Jesus God and Holy Spirit, to LIVE YOUR LIFE THROUGH ME, UNCEASINGLY, INCREASINGLY, FROM NOW ON, IN EVERY CIRCUMSTANCE. AMEN!! AMEN.

I also pledge myself to work with You, Dear Lord God, to get this Secret out:
    To as many people as possible,
      In as many places as possible,
        By as many methods as is possible,
          As quickly as possible!!! Amen.

I thank You, Yahshua Jesus, for taking me with You, when You raised up from the Tomb, and You took me with You when You ascended up to Heaven (Eph.1:20,21 & 2:4-6, Ps.16 & 91, Col.3) and with You when You sat down at the Heavenly Father, Papa Yahweh's right hand, on His Throne! I thank You that I am seated now in You, Jesus, here in the Throne-Room of my Heavenly Father. Whether asleep or awake, I'm here - on Your lap, in Your arms, listening to Your heart-beat, Your whispers of encouragement and love and guidance.

From now on, please always live Your Life through me. Speak Your words through me. Be all that You are, in me, all the time, now, and forever more. In Jesus' Yahshua's Name. Amen.

"AS CHRIST IS - SO ARE WE - IN THIS WORLD"!!   1 John 4:17b

Who would dare to put an upper limit on the marvelous possibilities of this spectacular truth!, this "Mystery of the Gospel of the Ages", this "King's Greatest Secret"!!

"AS CHRIST IS - SO ARE WE - IN THIS WORLD"!!   1 John 4:17b

In the Almighty Name of Yahweh Yahshua Jesus Christ The Righteous, we insist that this Truth not be limited! Look at the previous list of Scriptures again. Here are only a few, in closing:

1) "I can do ALL things through Christ Who strengthens me." Phil.4:13
2) "We - - are transformed into God's VERY SAME IMAGE"!!!! 2 Cor.3:18
3) "The works that I do, shall you do, and greater works than these, shall you do."!! John 14:4
4) We can walk, "Even as He (Jesus) walks"!! 1 John 2:6
5) "As Christ is, SO ARE WE, in this World"!! 1 John 4:17b

"Now, unto Him Who is able to keep you from falling (or stumbling), and to present you faultless, before the Presence of His Glory, with exceeding joy, to the Only Wise God, Our Savior, be Glory, and Majesty, Dominion and Power, now and forever. - Amen!"

Review Questions:

1) Is it possible to live without sinning? (Explain)

2) What, of ours, did Jesus take with Him, to the Cross?

3) What is the King's Greatest Secret?

4) What is the difference between Christ helping you do or speak good things, and Him doing the speaking or doing through you?

5) Why was it necessary for Christ to take you with Him to the Cross?

6) Without practical revelation understanding of "the King's Greatest Secret", has positive thinking got much power?

7) Why is suicide not necessary? Because Christ lovingly killed your self, softly, already, at the Cross! Then, He raised you up in newness of Life, and is now available to live His glorious Life, through you! Will you let Him?!

8) The following phrases go with what Bible verse references? (You may look them up, from the reference list, below).

Victory • Victory, always, everywhere • Free from sin • Risen with Christ our Life • Seated in Christ • Fulness of joy • _____ unspeakable • We've been blest with every blessing • Joy of the Lord is our Strength •

Joy unspeakable • Secret Place of the Most High • Every blessing • Joy of the Lord, our Strength • Mind of Christ • Can do all things through Christ • We can walk blamelessly • All power and authority • We are the light of the world • To live = Christ • All, all, always abounding • Whatever we ask • Abundant Life • All things for Life • More than conquerors • We are as He is • All things are possible • Know the Mysteries of the Kingdom • Walk as Jesus walked • Greatest Mystery in History • I can look like Jesus • For me to live IS Christ • Christ IS my Wisdom, my Salvation • I have been crucified with Christ, • and it is no longer I who live, • BUT CHRIST LIVES IN ME • CHRIST IS OUR LIFE • As He (Christ) is, SO ARE **WE**

1 Cor.15:57, 2 Cor.2:14-16, Rom.6:6-22, Col.3:1-3, Eph.2:6, Ps.16:11, 1 Pet.1:8, Ps.91, Eph.1:3-4, Neh.8:10, 1 Cor.2:16, Phil.4:13, Jude 24, Mt.28:18, Mt.5:14, Phil.1:21, 2 Cor.9:8, John 14:13, John 10:10, 2 Pet.1:1-4, Rom.8:37, Mt.19:26, Luke 8:10, 1 John 2:6, Col.1:25-29, 1 Cor.1:30, 2 Cor.3:18, Galatians 2:20, 1 Cor.2:1, 1 John 4:17b

9) Gal.2:20 - Are you living?

10) Can we be perfect? If not, why? If so, how?

11) What did Jesus mean when He said, "Be

perfect"?

12) What is the false doctrine of "Sinless Perfection"?

13) What is the main solution for most arguments about the Bible?

14) How is calling "idealistic", what God calls "necessary', "practical", "available" and "attainable", calling God a liar??

15) What 3 steps are necessary for Christ to be to the maximum in our life?

16) Do you have the mind of Christ?

17) In the Word, what's the main evidence, sign, fruit, or proof that you are full of God?

18) Not, "Have you been filled with", but, "are you full of God right now"? (Give yourself a percentage.)

19) What would happen to a clean and freshly sacrificed (killed) lamb under the hot Israel sun, if nothing more happened, after it was killed?

20) What else is necessary?

21) What is this symbolic of?

22) Who should praise the Lord with shouting and clapping? (Psalm 47)

23) Why can we have an experience MORE REAL than if we fell dead, and Christ was

looking around for a fresh warm dead body He could move into and raise up and BECOME the Life of, living on Earth again - disguised as you? In this case, we participate in the adventure!

24) Who is the grasshopper - elephant in the illustration?

25) What is the main difference between Christ helping us do or be something and Him being or doing it in and through you?

26) Are we supposed to discipline the old nature, the old man, or the old self?

27) Does Christ want there to be any difference between Who He is at the Father's right hand, and Who He is - in you?

28) Are you also willing to teach others to teach others how to share this "Secret"?

29) If you devoted the rest of your life to sharing this "Secret", would your life have been, "well lived"?

30) WILL YOU???????

31) Would you be willing by means of your gracious giving, to help us reach others through the printing of more of these small books?

CONCLUSION

What would Jesus do, if He were my Life?

PRETEND WITH ME FOR A MOMENT, THAT JESUS CHRIST IS YOUR LIFE!!! What would Jesus do, if HE were reigning and ruling as King, President, and Lord, upon the throne of YOUR life? What if Jesus were living again on the Earth, having come, in that fourth way, having come into our hearts to reign as King from the throne of our heart - not just as resident, within, but also, as President of the World, THROUGH us!!

Lean back in your easy chair, and pretend with me: Let's pretend that Jesus returns to be the King of the Earth. The way He decided to do it this time, was, at your invitation, to take over your body, your tongue, your conscious mind, (although you would still be conscious, and still be able to kick Christ out, or to limit His Life in you to any or every extent, or, you could let Him rule to His heart's content!!!) What would Jesus do, through you?! What would Jesus say, through you? How would Jesus act, through you? What would His attitude be, in you? How would Jesus, through you, treat others?

What if Jesus became the Life of one of the Dear Ones, and you mistreated that person? IT WOULD BE CREDITED TO YOUR ACCOUNT, AS HAVING BEEN DONE TO JESUS!

Let's let Jesus live His glorified, risen, powerful, lovely Life - through us, AS OUR LIFE!!! Amen?!

Have you learned "the Secret"??! Simply reckon, consider, and act as though it is true, because it **is** true, that you have been crucified with Christ, crucified, killed, dead, and buried with Christ. Then, see yourself as having been raised up with Jesus Christ, in newness of Life - forgiven, raised, ascended, glorified and seated IN Jesus Christ, at the Father's right hand! From now on, you are to do everything in Life, from a "Throne-Room Mentality". Psalm 91, Psalm 16, etc. "I have set Yahweh, the Lord, always before me. Because He is at my right hand, I shall not be moved." "He that dwelleth in the Secret Place of the Most High, shall abide under the Shadow of the Almighty." "In Thy Presence is fullness of joy, at Thy right hand, there are pleasures, forevermore."!!! Col. 3:3 "For ye are dead, and your life is hid with Christ in God."

GLORY

Remember when Jesus took the children up in His arms and blessed them? Ephesians 1 & 2, especially 2:6 tells us where we are: That Father Yahweh "hath raised us up, together with Christ, and made us all sit together in the Heavenly Places innnnn Christ Jesus" Baptism by immersion signifies that WE WENT WITH JESUS into His crucifixion, death, burial, resurrection, ascension AND GLORIFICATION!!! Romans 8:30 says that those "whom He justified, He also glorified."!

The Bible tells us that we are, right NOW, SEATED IN JESUS CHRIST at the Father's right hand. Here we are, on the Throne with our Heavenly Father, with Christ AS our Life! God wants us to live here, never to leave, never to have another mentality or way of thinking, than a gloriously victorious "Throne-Room Mentality".

Can you picture yourself going with Jesus to the Cross, to the grave, to the skies?!!! Can you see yourself crawling up into your Heavenly Father's lap - "Underneath, are the Everlasting Arms"!!, and putting your ear up against the Heavenly Father's heart of Love, and listening to God's heart-beat - His whispers of encouragement?!!! We can look like He looks - 2 Cor.3:18. We can walk like He walks - 1 John 2:6. We can be as He is - 1 John 4:17. You never need to leave your Heavenly Daddy Yahweh's Lap, His Arms, His Throne, His Presence, His Glory, or His Anointing. (He IS our Anointing!) From now on, and you don't need to wait until after you die!!!, Jesus can ALWAYS be your Life!! You can always be seated on the Throne, IN Him, at Papa God's right hand, ruling and reigning with Him, forever and forever! WOW! What a glorious Secret!! Looking like Jesus, talking like Jesus, thinking, being like Jesus - because Jesus has now become - your Life!!! And we all lived **HAPPILY EVER AFTER!!!!** May you live happily every after, with Jesus Christ AAAAAAS YOUR LIFE!!! In Jesus' Name! Amen.

"I'VE BEEN KILLED!"

What would you think, if I, as a stranger, testified, "I've been murdered, martyred, maimed and massacred. But I'm alive!" And, then, I told you that it's not really me that's living. What would you think? Yet, this is EXACTLY what the Apostle Paul was saying in Galatians 2:20! We discover that it was NOT Paul who wrote his epistles, nor went on his missionary trips, but it was Jesus Christ, disguised as Paul, Who wrote and traveled. Likewise, the Glorified Christ wants to do His miracles through you, speaking, living, thinking, being, loving - through YOU!!! John 14:10 says, "Believest thou not, that I am in the Father, and the Father in Me? The words that I speak unto you, I speak not of Myself: but the Father That dwelleth in Me, He doeth the works." See? Christ did not do the miracles, signs and wonders, but the Father did the miracles through Him, exactly the way Creator King of Everything wants to live His glorified Life - through you!!! Will you let Him???!

A GREAT MIRACULOUS MYSTERY!!!

2 Chronicles 2:6 and 2 Chronicles 6:18 tell us that the entire Universe cannot contain God, for God is too big!!! Yet, on the other hand, Ephesians 3:19b tells us that we can be fillllled with allll the fullllness of God!! Think of it, meditate on it, marvel at it, experience it, live with it and in it, that, though the Universe cannot contain God, yet, your brain can, your head can, your skin can, your cells can, your muscles can, your bones can, your hands can, your body can contain alllll the fulllllness of God!!!!!!!!!!!!! Please, always sweetly allow God

the Father, God the Son and God the Holy Spirit to occupy every part of you, to live His Glorious Life through you, unhindered, increasingly, unceasingly, now and forever more. Amen.

Welcome now, and evermore, to this lovely

KING'S GREATEST SECRET!!!

CHEERFUL GIVING

Very, very few have ever responded to this offer, this page, but we are pleading with you to carefully, prayerfully consider this:

We love to live to give. We have given literally tens of thousands of these little books away. If you cannot afford to buy these truths, we want you to have them anyway, so please do not be embarrassed to ask for these books for free. Yet, we know that you may enjoy giving, as well.

Would you enjoy entering with us into a lovely adventure of giving to see this message and these books given to multitudes of Dear Ones, in near and distant places, who may not be able to contribute? Right now, we desperately need to print or reprint every one of our books and articles. If you want to help us fulfill the Great Commission, and be one of The Great Commission Ministries with us, your loving gifts and donations, alms and love offerings will be most appreciated.

Your tax deductible gifts to us will enable us to print and explode these truths to many dear ones!!! Will you, won't you, can you help us preach this Gospel of the Kingdom, in near and distant places, through your giving?!! Send your tax-deductible love offerings to us at Great Commission Ministries, 9473 Co. Rd. D, Webster, WI 54893. This will enable us to stay in print, for Jesus' sake. Thank you!!!

www.Great-Commission-Ministries.org
Email: gcmco77@yahoo.com

WE LOVE YOU!!!

The Circle of God's Arms

(An invitation to greater intimacy with God)
by john roy bohlen & John 5:30

My <u>child</u>, I stand <u>here</u>
    With My <u>arms</u> open <u>wide</u>,
Saying, "<u>Prec</u>ious, come <u>near</u>,
    And <u>sit</u> by My <u>side</u>."
        You <u>don't</u> need to <u>wait</u>, dear,
            Till <u>after</u> you've <u>died</u>.

This <u>place</u> on My <u>throne</u>
    Is re<u>served</u> just for <u>you</u>
I <u>a</u>lways have <u>known</u>
    Where we have <u>int</u>imacy <u>true</u>

Reign <u>with</u> Me on <u>high</u>
    Far a<u>bove</u> every <u>foe</u>,
Come <u>here</u> and draw <u>nigh</u>
    With all <u>else</u> far be<u>low</u>.

Come <u>here</u>, feel My <u>whisk</u>ers,
    With your <u>ear</u>, hear My <u>whisp</u>ers.
Draw <u>near</u> to My <u>chest</u>,
    It is <u>here</u> you'll find <u>rest</u>!

With your <u>ear</u>, hear My <u>heart</u> beat.
    Come <u>near</u>, take your <u>own</u> seat.
I'm <u>glad</u> that I <u>found</u> you,
    Not <u>sad</u> that I <u>crowned</u> you.

You can <u>live</u> 'neath My <u>wings</u>.
    Over <u>you</u> My heart <u>sings</u>,
Gone are <u>all</u> life's a<u>larms</u>
    In the <u>circle</u> of <u>My</u> arms.

YOUR HEART - OUR HOME!

by John Roy Bohlen & John 5:30 - February. 1998

I love You, Papa Yahweh, with all my heart.
    With all my soul, with every part.
My heart pours out strong love for Thee
    My thanks pours out, eternally.

Your flow of grace enables me,
    To follow strongly after Thee.
        To yearn for Thee quite earnestly.
I'm basking in Your Presence now,
    This sweet tranquility makes me bow.

We live far over everything,
    We reign serene here with our King.
This is our home, we need not leave,
    But ever close, to Thee we cleave.

Not, "Help us live", but, "Be our Life!"
    Oh, live through us, there is no strife.
Speak through our lips, bless through our hands.
    Walk through our feet, through many lands.

We're listening to Your heart beat,
    Upon Your lap we take our seat.
Never to leave here, never to roam
    Snuggling close, Your arms are our home.

Beneath Your wings I take my place,
    Beneath Your feathers, I find grace.
Within Your Shadow, You Most High,
    We never need to say "Good bye."

A poem to the Father by John.

AMAZING!

by john roy bohlen & John 5:30

November 18, 2004

An amazing thing,
Makes my heart sing!
Christ living in me.
To God I cling.
Let joy bells ring.
God is living in me.

I'm saved from Hell.
Emmanuel.
Creator of All.
Saved from the Fall.

He knows my name.
Within He came.
I'm filled with bliss.
God gives a kiss.

Abundant Life.
There's no more strife.
No more fears.
God lives between my ears.

Creator of All,
I stand in awe.
I can't but win.
God, inside my skin.

All sin erase.
He took my place
God behind my face.
Amazing grace!

I LOVE YOU!

Dear Darling Daddy Yahweh, I love You!
    And, Precious Holy Spirit, I love You, too!
Lovely Mighty Jesus, You are my Friend,
    God, You're in me! What a perfect blend!

I can look into the mirror, and what do I see?
    I can see Yahshua, looking back at me?
Because I am so great? Not on your life!
    God has filled me full of Him, now there's no more strife.

You see, if you invite Jesus, to come and live within,
    He will save you from Hell-fire, He will take away all sin.
Ask Him to be your Life. Ask Him to be your Lord.
    Your humblest prayer, you will not be ignored.

But if you will not ask Him in, He surely will stay out,
    He won't impose Himself on you. Of this there is no doubt.
You must give your whole life to Him, all that you posses.
    And Christ will give His All to you, your whole life He will bless.

So let Him be His Own Self in you,
    Let Him walk around in your shoes.
Let Christ bless through your hands,
    Let Him speak through your lips,
        Through you, let Him spread the Good News.

The whole of the Christian Life can be summed
    Everything can be told, think it true:
Sweetly rest your whole life in the Arms of the Father,
    And let Christ live His whole Life, through you!"
        by John Roy Bohlen & John 5:30 - 1997

SECRET POEM

If I were to tell the most important story,
    'Twould be "Christ In You, the Hope of Glory"!
What does this mean? This seems almost strange.
    This is Truth's gleam - Love's brightest page.

If you were to ask, "What is the most important thing?"
    The Light would flash, the bell would ring.
"God comes, lives in you, at your request,
    Makes Himself known, helps pass the Test."

Creator of Everything, Lord of this Earth,
    Cosmos King, He gives all, birth.
He is Friend to all who see His worth.
    Out of sadness, He brings mirth.

When He died there on the Cross,
    He saved you from all loss.
He took your sins and sicknesses,
    Took your whole life and lifelessness.

When He went there, He took you.
    Every weakness, He took, too.
Inadequacy, inferiority, inability.
    Incapacity, insecurity, instability.

So, now the time has come to live,
    So let Christ live His Life through you!
He will bestow all He can give.
    Be Friend and Provider, all life through!

To have You live through us, Oh what delight!
    To shine with Your Glory, Oh what a sight!
To move in Your power, channels of Your might!
    Everyone who is willing, You lovingly invite.

To have You bless through our hands,
> You walk through our feet.
> To have You speak through our lips
> > to all that we meet.

Residing in You, our life is complete.
> Abiding in You, nothing could be more sweet.

Enjoying Your greatness, in all that we do.
> Enjoying Your sweetness, all our lives through.

Our home is Your Presence, this is so true.
> Not a stitch of the old life, every thing new.

The Throne-Room perspective - Wow! What a view!
> Whew! More fun than the zoo!

All who are willing, to Your bosom drew.
> God's arms are out stretched, there's room for you, too.

by John Roy Bohlen, Good Friday, his mother's birthday, 1997 the day before they left on their Spring ministry trip.

Please memorize and remember this very important sentence:

"There is nothing more to do, than to relax in the loving arms of my Heavenly Father, and let Christ live His glorified Life, through me."

CONTACT INFORMATION

You may contact us at:

Great Commission Ministries
9473 County Road D
Webster, WI 54893

Phone: 715-866-4060
email: gcmco77@yahoo.com

Other books and articles we have written:

<u>How To Rule The World</u>, or Seek 1st the Kingdom of God
<u>The Cult of Cannibals</u>, or, How To Rightly Relate
<u>The Sexual Ministry</u>, or, How To Live Happily Ever After (Our book on marriage)
<u>How To Raise 'Purfect' Kids</u>
<u>The King's Greatest Secret!</u>
<u>FGM</u>, or Female Circumcision
<u>Poetry</u>
<u>Law, Grace and Law</u>
<u>Body Stewardship</u>
<u>The Glorious Church</u>
<u>Apostles</u>: Who, How, What, When and Where
<u>True African Adventure Stories</u>
<u>What is God's Name?</u>
<u>Dancing On The Water</u> - A Family Autobiography

**Website: www.Great-Commission-Ministries.org
Or, simply google: John Roy Bohlen**

WE LOVE YOU ! ! !